POETRY FROM CRESCENT MOON

William Shakespeare: *Selected Sonnets and Verse*
edited, with an introduction by Mark Tuley

William Shakespeare: *The Sonnets*
edited and introduced by Mark Tuley

*Shakespeare: Love, Poetry and Magic
in Shakespeare's Sonnets and Plays*
by B.D. Barnacle

Edmund Spenser: *Heavenly Love: Selected Poems*
selected and introduced by Teresa Page

Robert Herrick: *Delight In Disorder: Selected Poems*
edited and introduced by M.K. Pace

Sir Thomas Wyatt: *Love For Love: Selected Poems*
selected and introduced by Louise Cooper

John Donne: *Air and Angels: Selected Poems*
selected and introduced by A.H. Ninham

D.H. Lawrence: *Being Alive: Selected Poems*
edited with an introduction by Margaret Elvy

*D.H. Lawrence: Symbolic Landscapes*
by Jane Foster

*D.H. Lawrence: Infinite Sensual Violence*
by M.K. Pace

Percy Bysshe Shelley: *Paradise of Golden Lights: Selected Poems*
selected and introduced by Charlotte Greene

Thomas Hardy: *Her Haunting Ground: Selected Poems*
edited, with an introduction by A.H. Ninham

*Sexing Hardy: Thomas Hardy and Feminism*
by Margaret Elvy

Emily Bronte: *Darkness and Glory: Selected Poems*
selected and introduced by Miriam Chalk

John Keats: *Bright Star: Selected Poems*
edited with an introduction by Miriam Chalk

Henry Vaughan: *A Great Ring of Pure and Endless Light: Selected Poems*
selected and introduced by A.H. Ninham

*The Crescent Moon Book of Love Poetry*
edited by Louise Cooper

*The Crescent Moon Book of Mystical Poetry in English*
edited by Carol Appleby

*The Crescent Moon Book of Nature Poetry From Langland to Lawrence*
edited by Margaret Elvy

*The Crescent Moon Book of Metaphysical Poetry*
edited and introduced by Charlotte Greene

*The Crescent Moon Book of Elizabethan Love Poetry*
edited and introduced by Carol Appleby

*The Crescent Moon Book of Romantic Poetry*
edited and introduced by L.M. Poole

*Blinded By Her Light The Love-Poetry of Robert Graves*
by Jeremy Mark Robinson

*The Best of Peter Redgrove's Poetry: The Book of Wonders*
by Peter Redgrove, edited and introduced by Jeremy Mark Robinson

*Peter Redgrove: Here Comes the Flood*
by Jeremy Mark Robinson

*Sex-Magic-Poetry-Cornwall: A Flood of Poems*
by Peter Redgrove, edited with an essay by Jeremy Mark Robinson

*Brigitte's Blue Heart*
by Jeremy Reed

*Claudia Schiffer's Red Shoes*
by Jeremy Reed

*By-Blows: Uncollected Poems*
by D.J. Enright

*Petrarch, Dante and the Troubadours: The Religion of Love and Poetry*
by Cassidy Hughes

Dante: *Selections From the Vita Nuova*
translated by Thomas Okey

Arthur Rimbaud: *Selected Poems*
edited and translated by Andrew Jary

Arthur Rimbaud: *A Season in Hell*
edited and translated by Andrew Jary

*Rimbaud: Arthur Rimbaud and the Magic of Poetry*
by Jeremy Mark Robinson

Friedrich Hölderlin: *Hölderlin's Songs of Light: Selected Poems*
translated by Michael Hamburger

Rainer Maria Rilke: *Dance the Orange:* Selected Poems
translated by Michael Hamburger

*Rilke: Space, Essence and Angels in the Poetry of Rainer Maria Rilke*
by B.D. Barnacle

*German Romantic Poetry: Goethe, Novalis,
Heine, Hölderlin, Schlegel, Schiller*
by Carol Appleby

Arseny Tarkovsky: *Life, Life: Selected Poems*
translated by Virginia Rounding

Emily Dickinson: *Wild Nights: Selected Poems*
selected and introduced by Miriam Chalk

*Cavafy: Anatomy of a Soul*
by Matt Crispin

# Amoretti

# Amoretti

# Edmund Spenser

Edited by Teresa Page

CRESCENT MOON

CRESCENT MOON PUBLISHING
P.O. Box 1312, Maidstone
Kent, ME14 5XU
Great Britain, www.crmoon.com

First published 2007.

Printed and bound in the U.S.A.
Set in Garamond Book 12 on 16pt.
Designed by Radiance Graphics.

The right of Teresa Page to be identified as the editor of this book has been asserted generally in accordance with sections 77 and 78 of the Copyright, Designs and Patents Act 1988.

All rights reserved. No part of this book may be reprinted or reproduced, stored in a retrieval system, or transmitted, in any form or by any means, electronic, mechanical, photocopying, recording or otherwise, without permission from the publisher.

*British Library Cataloguing in Publication data*
*Spenser, Edmund*
*Amoretti. - (British Poets Series)*
*I. Title II. Page, Teresa*
*III. Series*
*821.3*

*ISBN-13 9781861711533*

## *CONTENTS*

Amoretti     15

Note and Further Reading     105

Edmund Spenser

# AMORETTI
## AND
## Epithalamion.

*Written not long since
by Edmunde
Spenser.*

Printed for William
Ponsonby. 1595.

AMORETTI

WRITTEN NOT LONG SINCE BY

EDMUNDE SPENSER.


PRINTED FOR WILLIAM POSBONBY.

1595.

## G. W. SENIOR

## TO THE AUTHOR.

Darke is the day when Phoebus face is shrowded,
And weaker sights may wander soone astray;
But when they see his glorious raies unclowded,
With steddy steps they keepe the perfect way:
So, while this Muse in forraine land doth stay,
Invention weepes, and pennes are cast aside;
The time, like night, deprivd of chearfull day;
And few doe write, but ah! too soone may slide.
Then his thee home, that art our perfect guide,
And with thy wit illustrate Englands fame,
Daunting therby our neighbors ancient pride,
That do for Poesie challenge chiefest name:
    So we that live, and ages that succeed,
      With great applause thy learned works shall reed.

Ah! Colin, whether on the lowly plaine,
Piping to shepheards thy sweet roundelayes,
Or whether singing, in some loftie vaine,
Heroicke deeds of past or present dayes,
Or whether in thy lovely mistresse praise
Thou list to exercise thy learned quill,
Thy Muse hath got such grace and power to please,
With rare invention, beautified by skill,
As who therin can ever ioy their fill!
O, therefore let that happy Muse proceed
To clime the height of Vertues sacred hill,
Where endlesse honour shal be made thy meed:
  Because no malice of succeeding dales
  Can rase those records of thy lasting praise.


G. W. I (Junior)

# AMORETTI

I

Happy, ye leaves! when as those lilly hands
Which hold my life in their dead-doing might
Shall handle you, and hold in loves soft bands,
Lyke captives trembling at the victors sight.
And happy lines! on which, with starry light,
Those lamping eyes will deigne sometimes to look,
And reade the sorrowes of my dying spright,
And happy rymes! bath'd in the sacred brooke
Of Helicon, whence she derived is.
When ye behold that Angels blessed looke,
My soules long-lacked food, my heavens blis,
    Leaves, lines, and rymes, seeke her to please alone,
    Whom if ye please, I care for other none!

II

Unquiet thought! whom at the first I bred
Of th'inward bale of my love-pined hart,
And sithens have with sighes and sorrowes fed,
Till greater then my wombe thou woxen art,
Breake forth at length out of the inner part,
In which thou lurkest lyke to vipers brood,
And seeke some succour both to ease my smart,
And also to sustayne thy selfe with food.
But if in presence of that fayrest Proud
Thou chance to come, fall lowly at her feet;
And with meek humblesse and afflicted mood
Pardon for thee, and grace for me, intreat:
    Which if she graunt, then live, and my love cherish:
    If not, die soone, and I with thee will perish.

III

The soverayne beauty which I do admyre,
Witnesse the world how worthy to be prayzed!
The light wherof hath kindled heavenly fyre
In my fraile spirit, by her from basenesse raysed;
That being now with her huge brightnesse dazed,
Base thing I can no more endure to view:
But, looking still on her, I stand amazed
At wondrous sight of so celestiall hew.
So when my toung would speak her praises dew,
It stopped is with thoughts astonishment;
And when my pen would write her titles true,
It ravisht is with fancies wonderment:
    Yet in my hart I then both speak and write
    The wonder that my wit cannot endite.

# IV

New yeare, forth looking out of Ianus gate,
Doth seeme to promise hope of new delight,
And, bidding th'old adieu, his passed date
Bids all old thoughts to die in dumpish spright;
And calling forth out of sad Winters night
Fresh Love, that long hath slept in cheerlesse bower,
Wils him awake, and soone about him dight
His wanton wings and darts of deadly power.
For lusty Spring now in his timely howre
Is ready to come forth, him to receive;
And warns the Earth with divers colord flowre
To decke hir selfe, and her faire mantle weave.
    Then you, faire flowre! in whom fresh youth doth raine,
  Prepare your selfe new love to entertaine.

## V

Rudely thou wrongest my deare harts desire,
In finding fault with her too portly pride:
The thing which I doo most in her admire,
Is of the world unworthy most envide.
For in those lofty lookes is close implide
Scorn of base things, and sdeigne of foul dishonor;
Thretning rash eyes which gaze on her so wide,
That loosely they ne dare to looke upon her.
Such pride is praise, such portlinesse is honor,
That boldned innocence beares in hir eyes,
And her faire countenaunce, like a goodly banner,
Spreds in defiaunce of all enemies.
    Was never in this world ought worthy tride,
    Without some spark of such self-pleasing pride.

## VI

Be nought dismayd that her unmoved mind
Doth still persist in her rebellious pride:
Such love, not lyke to lusts of baser kynd,
The harder wonne, the firmer will abide.
The durefull oake whose sap is not yet dride
Is long ere it conceive the kindling fyre;
But when it once doth burne, it doth divide
Great heat, and makes his flames to heaven aspire.
So hard it is to kindle new desire
In gentle brest, that shall endure for ever:
Deepe is the wound that dints the parts entire
With chaste affects, that naught but death can sever.
    Then thinke not long in taking litle paine
    To knit the knot that ever shall remaine.

## VII

Fayre eyes! the myrrour of my mazed hart,
What wondrous vertue is contayn'd in you,
The which both lyfe and death forth from you dart
Into the obiect of your mighty view?
For when ye mildly looke with lovely hew,
Then is my soule with life and love inspired:
But when ye lowre, or looke on me askew,
Then do I die, as one with lightning fyred.
But since that lyfe is more then death desyred,
Looke ever lovely, as becomes you best;
That your bright beams, of my weak eyes admyred,
May kindle living fire within my brest.
    Such life should be the honor of your light,
    Such death the sad ensample of your might.

## VIII

More then most faire, full of the living fire
Kindled above unto the Maker nere,
No eyes, but joyes, in which al powers conspire,
That to the world naught else be counted deare!
Thrugh your bright beams doth not the blinded guest
Shoot out his darts to base affections wound;
But angels come, to lead fraile mindes to rest
In chast desires, on heavenly beauty bound.
You frame my thoughts, and fashion me within;
You stop my toung, and teach my hart to speake;
You calme the storme that passion did begin,
Strong thrugh your cause, but by your vertue weak.
    Dark is the world where your light shined never;
    Well is he borne that may behold you ever.

## IX

Long-while I sought to what I might compare
Those powrefull eyes which lighten my dark spright;
Yet find I nought on earth, to which I dare
Resemble th'ymage of their goodly light.
Not to the sun, for they doo shine by night;
Nor to the moone, for they are changed never;
Nor to the starres, for they have purer sight;
Nor to the fire, for they consume not ever;
Nor to the lightning, for they still persever;
Nor to the diamond, for they are more tender;
Nor unto cristall, for nought may them sever;
Nor unto glasse, such basenesse mought offend her.
    Then to the Maker selfe they likest be,
        Whose light doth lighten all that here we see.

## X

Unrighteous Lord of love, what law is this,
That me thou makest thus tormented be,
The whiles she lordeth in licentious blisse
Of her freewill, scorning both thee and me?
See! how the Tyrannesse doth joy to see
The hugh massacres which her eyes do make,
And humbled harts brings captive unto thee,
That thou of them mayst mightie vengeance take.
But her proud hart doe thou a little shake,
And that high look, with which she doth comptroll
All this worlds pride, bow to a baser make,
And al her faults in thy black booke enroll:
    That I may laugh at her in equall sort
    As she doth laugh at me, and makes my pain her
                        sport.

## XI

Dayly when I do seeke and sew for peace,
And hostages doe offer for ray truth,
She, cruell warriour, doth her selfe addresse
To battell, and the weary war renew'th;
Ne wilbe moov'd, with reason or with rewth,
To graunt small respit to my restlesse toile;
But greedily her fell intent poursewth,
Of my poore life to make unpittied spoile.
Yet my poore life, all sorrowes to assoyle,
I would her yield, her wrath to pacify;
But then she seeks, with torment and turmoyle,
To force me live, and will not let me dy.
    All paine hath end, and every war hafh peace;
    But mine, no price nor prayer may surcease.

## XII

One day I sought with her hart-thrilling eyes
To make a truce, and termes to entertaine;
All fearlesse then of so false enimies,
Which sought me to entrap in treasons traine.
So, as I then disarmed did remaine,
A wicked ambush, which lay hidden long
In the close covert of her guilful eyen,
Thence breaking forth, did thick about me throng.
Too feeble I t'abide the brunt so strong,
Was forst to yield my selfe into their hands;
Who, me captiving streight with rigorous wrong,
Have ever since kept me in cruell bands.
    So, Ladie, now to you I doo complaine
    Against your eyes, that iustice I may gaine.

## XIII

In that proud port which her so goodly graceth,
Whiles her faire face she reares up to the skie,
And to the ground her eie-lids low embaseth,
Most goodly temperature ye may descry;
Myld humblesse mixt with awful! maiestie.
For, looking on the earth whence she was borne,
Her minde remembreth her mortalitie,
Whatso is fayrest shall to earth returne.
But that same lofty countenance seemes to scorne
Base thing, and thinke how she to heaven may clime;
Treading downe earth as lothsome and forlorne,
That hinders heavenly thoughts with drossy slime.
    Yet lowly still vouchsafe to looke on me;
    Such lowlinesse shall make you lofty be.

## XIV

Retourne agayne, my forces late dismayd,
Unto the siege by you abandon'd quite.
Great shame it is to leave, like one afrayd,
So fayre a peece for one repulse so light.
'Gaynst such strong castles needeth greater might
Then those small forts which ye were wont belay:
Such haughty mynds, enur'd to hardy fight,
Disdayne to yield unto the first assay.
Bring therefore all the forces that ye may,
And lay incessant battery to her heart;
Playnts, prayers, vowes, ruth, sorrow, and dismay;
Those engins can the proudest love convert:
    And, if those fayle, fall down and dy before her;
    So dying live, and living do adore her.

## XV

Ye tradefull Merchants, that, with weary toyle,
Do seeke most pretious things to make your gain,
And both the Indias of their treasure spoile,
What needeth you to seeke so farre in vaine?
For loe, my Love doth in her selfe containe
All this worlds riches that may farre be found:
If saphyres, loe, her eyes be saphyres plaine;
If rubies, loe, hir lips be rubies sound;
If pearles, hir teeth be pearles, both pure and round;
If yvorie, her forhead yvory weene;
If gold, her locks are finest gold on ground;
If silver, her faire hands are silver sheene:
    But that which fairest is but few behold:-
    Her mind adornd with vertues manifold.

## XVI

One day as I unwarily did gaze
On those fayre eyes, my loves immortall light,
The whiles my stonisht hart stood in amaze,
Through sweet illusion of her lookes delight,
I mote perceive how, in her glauncing sight,
Legions of Loves with little wings did fly,
Darting their deadly arrows, fyry bright,
At every rash beholder passing by.
One of those archers closely I did spy,
Ayming his arrow at my very hart:
When suddenly, with twincle of her eye,
The damzell broke his misintended dart.
    Had she not so doon, sure I had bene slayne;
    Yet as it was, I hardly scap't with paine.

## XVII

The glorious pourtraict of that angels face,
Made to amaze weake mens confused skil,
And this worlds worthlesse glory to embase,
What pen, what pencil!, can expresse her fill?
For though he colours could devize at will,
And eke his learned hand at pleasure guide,
Least, trembling, it his workmanship should spill,
Yet many wondrous things there are beside:
The sweet eye-glaunces, that like arrowes glide,
The charming smiles, that rob sence from the hart,
The lovely pleasance, and the lofty pride,
Cannot expressed be by any art.
    A greater craftsmans hand thereto doth neede,
    That can expresse the life of things indeed.

## XVIII

The rolling wheele that runneth often round,
The hardest steele, in tract of time doth teare:
And drizling drops, that often doe redound,
The firmest flint doth in continuance weare:
Yet cannot I, with many a drooping teare
And long intreaty, soften her hard hart,
That she will once vouchsafe my plaint to heare,
Or looke with pitty on my payneful smart.
But when I pleade, she bids me play my part;
And when I weep, she sayes, teares are but water;
And when I sigh, she sayes, I know the art;
And when I waile, she turnes hir selfe to laughter.
    So do I weepe, and wayle, and pleade in vaine,
      Whiles she as steele and flint doth still remayne.

## XIX

The merry cuckow, messenger of Spring,
His trompet shrill hath thrise already sounded.
That warnes al lovers wayte upon their king,
Who now is coming forth with girland crouned.
With noyse whereof the quyre of byrds resounded
Their anthemes sweet, devized of loves prayse,
That all the woods theyr ecchoes back rebounded,
As if they knew the meaning of their layes.
But mongst them all which did Loves honor rayse,
No word was heard of her that most it ought;
But she his precept proudly disobayes,
And doth his ydle message set at nought.
    Therefore, O Love, unlesse she turne to thee
    Ere cuckow end, let her a rebell be!

## XX

In vaine I seeke and sew to her for grace,
And doe myne humbled hart before her poure,
The whiles her foot she in my necke doth place,
And tread my life downe in the lowly floure.
And yet the lyon, that is lord of power,
And reigneth over every beast in field,
In his most pride disdeigneth to devoure
The silly lambe that to his might doth yield.
But she, more cruell and more salvage wylde
Than either lyon or the lyonesse,
Shames not to be with guiltlesse bloud defylde,
But taketh glory in her cruelnesse.
    Fayrer then fayrest! let none ever say
      That ye were blooded in a yeelded pray.

## XXI

Was it the worke of Nature or of Art,
Which tempred so the feature of her face,
That pride and meeknesse, mist by equall part,
Doe both appeare t'adorne her beauties grace?
For with mild pleasance, which doth pride displace,
She to her love doth lookers eyes allure;
And with stern countenance back again doth chace
Their looser lookes that stir up lustes impure.
With such strange termes her eyes she doth inure,
That with one looke she doth my life dismay,
And with another doth it streight recure:
Her smile me drawes; her frowne me drives away.
    Thus doth she traine and teach me with her lookes;
    Such art of eyes I never read in bookes!

## XXII

This holy season, fit to fast and pray,
Men to devotion ought to be inclynd:
Therefore, I lykewise, on so holy day,
For my sweet saynt some service fit will find.
Her temple fayre is built within my mind,
In which her glorious ymage placed is;
On which my thoughts doo day and night attend,
Lyke sacred priests that never thinke amisse.
There I to her, as th'author of my blisse,
Will builde an altar to appease her yre;
And on the same my hart will sacrifise,
Burning in flames of pure and chaste desyre:
    The which vouchsafe, O Goddesse, to accept,
    Amongst thy deerest relicks to be kept.

## XXIII

Penelope, for her Ulisses sake,
Deviz'd a web her wooers to deceave;
In which the worke that she all day did make,
The same at night she did againe unreave.
Such subtile craft my damzell doth conceave,
Th'importune suit of my desire to shonne:
For all that I in many dayes do weave,
In one short houre I find by her undonne.
So when I thinke to end that I begonne,
I must begin and never bring to end:
For with one looke she spils that long I sponne,
And with one word my whole years work doth rend.
    Such labour like the spyders web I fynd,
        Whose fruitlesse worke is broken with least wynd.

## XXIV

When I behold that beauties wonderment,
And rare perfection of each goodly part,
Of Natures skill the onely complement,
I honor and admire the Makers art.
But when I feele the bitter balefull smart
Which her fayre eyes unwares doe worke in mee,
That death out of theyr shiny beames doe dart,
I thinke that I a new Pandora see,
Whom all the gods in councell did agree
Into this sinfull world from heaven to send,
That she to wicked men a scourge should bee,
For all their faults with which they did offend.
    But since ye are my scourge, I will intreat
    That for my faults ye will me gently beat.

## XXV

How long shall this lyke-dying lyfe endure,
And know no end of her owne mysery,
But wast and weare away in termes unsure,
'Twixt feare and hope depending doubtfully!
Yet better were attonce to let me die,
And shew the last ensample of your pride,
Then to torment me thus with cruelty,
To prove your powre, which I too wel have tride.
But yet if in your hardned brest ye bide
A close intent at last to shew me grace,
Then all the woes and wrecks which I abide,
As meanes of blisse I gladly wil embrace;
    And wish that more and greater they might be,
    That greater meede at last may turne to mee.

## XXVI

Sweet is the rose, but growes upon a brere;
Sweet is the junipeer; but sharpe his bough;
Sweet is the eglantine, but pricketh nere;
Sweet is the firbloome, but his braunches rough;
Sweet is the cypresse, but his rynd is rough;
Sweet is the nut, but bitter is his pill;
Sweet is the broome-flowre, but yet sowre enough;
And sweet is moly, but his root is ill.
So every sweet with soure is tempred still,
That maketh it be coveted the more:
For easie things, that may be got at will,
Most sorts of men doe set but little store.
    Why then should I accompt of little paine,
    That endlesse pleasure shall unto me gaine!

## XXVII

Faire Proud! now tell me, why should faire be proud,
Sith all worlds glorie is but drosse uncleane,
And in the shade of death it selfe shall shroud,
However now thereof ye little weene!
That goodly idoll, now so gay beseene,
Shall doffe her fleshes borrowd fayre attyre,
And be forgot as it had never beene,
That many now much worship and admire!
Ne any then shall after it inquire,
Ne any mention shall thereof remaine,
But what this verse, that never shall expyre,
Shall to you purchas with her thankles pain!
    Faire! be no lenger proud of that shall perish,
    But that which shall you make immortall cherish.

## XVIII

The laurel-leafe which you this day doe weare
Gives me great hope of your relenting mynd:
For since it is the badge which I doe beare,
Ye, bearing it, doe seeme to me inclind.
The powre thereof, which ofte in me I find,
Let it likewise your gentle brest inspire
With sweet infusion, and put you in mind
Of that proud mayd whom now those leaves attyre:
Proud Daphne, scorning Phrebus lovely fyre,
On the Thessalian shore from him did flie;
For which the gods, in theyr revengefull yre,
Did her transforme into a laurell-tree.
    Then fly no more, fayre Love, from Phebus chace,
    But in your brest his leafe and love embrace.

## XXIX

See! how the stubborne damzell doth deprave
My simple meaning with disdaynfull scorne,
And by the bay which I unto her gave
Accoumpts my self her captive quite forlorne.
The bay, quoth she, is of the victours born,
Yielded them by the vanquisht as theyr meeds,
And they therewith doe poetes heads adorne,
To sing the glory of their famous deeds.
But sith she will the conquest challeng needs,
Let her accept me as her faithfull thrall;
That her great triumph, which my skill exceeds,
I may in trump of fame blaze over all.
    Then would I decke her head with glorious bayes,
    And fill the world with her victorious prayse.

## XXX

My Love is lyke to yse, and I to fyre:
How comes it then that this her cold so great
Is not dissolv'd through my so hot desyre,
But harder growes the more I her intreat?
Or how comes it that my exceeding heat
Is not delayd by her hart-frosen cold,
But that I burne much more in boyling sweat,
And feele my flames augmented manifold?
What more miraculous thing may be told,
That fire, which all things melts, should harden yse,
And yse, which is congeald with sencelesse cold,
Should kindle fyre by wonderful devyse?
    Such is the powre of love in gentle mind,
      That it can alter all the course of kynd.

## XXXI

Ah! why hath Nature to so hard a hart
Given so goodly giftes of beauties grace,
Whose pryde depraves each other better part,
And all those pretious ornaments deface?
Sith to all other beastes of bloody race
A dreadfull countenance she given hath,
That with theyr terrour all the rest may chace,
And warne to shun the daunger of theyr wrath.
But my proud one doth worke the greater scath,
Through sweet allurement of her lovely hew,
That she the better may in bloody bath
Of such poore thralls her cruell hands embrew.
    But did she know how ill these two accord,
    Such cruelty she would have soone abhord.

## XXXII

The paynefull smith with force of fervent heat
The hardest yron soone doth mollify,
That with his heavy sledge he can it beat,
And fashion to what he it list apply.
Yet cannot all these flames in which I fry
Her hart, more hard then yron, soft a whit,
Ne all the playnts and prayers with which I
Doe beat on th'andvile of her stubberne wit:
But still, the more she fervent sees my fit,
The more she frieseth in her wilfull pryde,
And harder growes, the harder she is smit
With all the playnts which to her be applyde.
    What then remaines but I to ashes burne,
    And she to stones at length all frosen turne!

## XXXIII

Great wrong I doe, I can it not deny,
To that most sacred empresse, my dear dred,
Not finishing her Queene of Faery,
That mote enlarge her living prayses, dead.
But Lodwick, this of grace to me aread:
Do ye not thinck th'accomplishment of it
Sufficient worke for one mans simple head,
All were it, as the rest, but rudely writ?
How then should I, without another wit,
Thinck ever to endure so tedious toyle,
Sith that this one is tost with troublous fit
Of a proud Love, that doth my spirite spoyle?
    Cease, then, till she vouchsafe to grawnt me rest,
    Or lend you me another living brest.

## XXXIV

Lyke as a ship, that through the ocean wyde
By conduct of some star doth make her way,
Whenas a storm hath dimd her trusty guyde,
Out of her course doth wander far astray,
So I, whose star, that wont with her bright ray
Me to direct, with cloudes is over-cast,
Doe wander now in darknesse and dismay,
Through hidden perils round about me plast.
Yet hope I well that, when this storme is past,
My Helice, the lodestar of ray lyfe,
Will shine again, and looke on me at last,
With lovely light to cleare my cloudy grief.
    Till then I wander carefull, comfortlesse,
      In secret sorrow and sad pensivenesse.

## XXXV

My hungry eyes, through greedy covetize
Still to behold the obiect of their paine,
With no contentment can themselves suffize;
But having, pine, and having not, complaine.
For lacking it, they cannot lyfe sustayne;
And having it, they gaze on it the more,
In their amazement lyke Narcissus vaine,
Whose eyes him starv'd: so plenty makes me poore.
Yet are mine eyes so filled with the store
Of that faire sight, that nothing else they brooke,
But lothe the things which they did like before,
And can no more endure on them to looke.
    All this worlds glory seemeth vayne to me,
    And all their showes but shadowes, saving she.

## XXXVI

Tell me, when shall these wearie woes have end;
Or shall their ruthlesse torment never cease,
But al my days in pining languor spend,
Without hope of asswagement or release?
Is there no meanes for me to purchace peace,
Or make agreement with her thrilling eyes;
But that their cruelty doth still increace,
And dayly more augment my miseryes?
But when ye have shew'd all extremityes,
Then think how little glory ye have gayned
By slaying him, whose lyfe, though ye despyse,
Mote have your life in honor long maintayned.
    But by his death, which some perhaps will mone,
    Ye shall condemned be of many a one.

## XXXVII

What guyle is this, that those her golden tresses
She doth attyre under a net of gold,
And with sly skill so cunningly them dresses,
That which is gold or haire may scarse be told?
Is it that mens frayle eyes, which gaze too bold,
She may entangle in that golden snare;
And, being caught, may craftily enfold
Their weaker harts, which are not wel aware?
Take heed therefore, myne eyes, how ye doe stare
Henceforth too rashly on that guilefull net,
In which if ever ye entrapped are,
Out of her bands ye by no meanes shall get.
    Fondnesse it were for any, being free,
      To covet fetters, though they golden bee!

## XXXVIII

Arion, when, through tempests cruel wracke,
He forth was thrown into the greedy seas,
Through the sweet musick which his harp did make
Allur'd a dolphin him from death to ease.
But my rude musick, which was wont to please
Some dainty eares, cannot, with any skill,
The dreadfull tempest of her wrath appease,
Nor move the dolphin from her stubborn will.
But in her pride she dooth persever still,
All carelesse how my life for her decayes:
Yet with one word she can it save or spill.
To spill were pitty, but to save were prayse!
    Chuse rather to be praysd for doing good,
      Then to be blam'd for spilling guiltlesse blood.

## XXXIX

Sweet smile! the daughter of the Queene of Love,
Expressing all thy mothers powrefull art,
With which she wonts to temper angry Iove,
When all the gods he threats with thundring dart,
Sweet is thy vertue, as thy selfe sweet art.
For when on me thou shinedst late in sadnesse,
A melting pleasance ran through every part,
And me revived with hart-robbing gladnesse;
Whylest rapt with joy resembling heavenly madnesse,
My soule was ravisht quite as in a traunce,
And, feeling thence no more her sorrowes sadnesse,
Fed on the fulnesse of that chearfull glaunce.
    More sweet than nectar, or ambrosiall meat,
    Seem'd every bit which thenceforth I did eat.

## XL

Mark when she smiles with amiable cheare,
And tell me whereto can ye lyken it;
When on each eyelid sweetly doe appeare
An hundred Graces as in shade to sit.
Lykest it seemeth, in my simple wit,
Unto the fayre sunshine in somers day,
That, when a dreadfull storme away is flit,
Thrugh the broad world doth spred his goodly ray
At sight whereof, each bird that sits on spray.
And every beast that to his den was fled,
Comes forth afresh out of their late dismay,
And to the light lift up their drouping hed.
    So my storme-beaten hart likewise is cheared
    With that sunshine, when cloudy looks are cleared.

## XLI

Is it her nature, or is it her will,
To be so cruell to an humbled foe?
If nature, then she may it mend with skill;
If will, then she at will may will forgoe.
But if her nature and her will be so,
That she will plague the man that loves her most,
And take delight t'encrease a wretches woe,
Then all her natures goodly guifts are lost;
And that same glorious beauties ydle boast
Is but a bayt such wretches to beguile,
As, being long in her loves tempest tost,
She meanes at last to make her pitious spoyle.
    O fayrest fayre! let never it be named,
    That so fayre beauty was so fowly shamed.

## XLII

The love which me so cruelly tormenteth
So pleasing is in my extreamest paine,
That, all the more my sorrow it augmenteth,
The more I love and doe embrace my bane.
Ne do I wish (for wishing were but vaine)
To be acquit fro my continual smart,
But joy her thrall for ever to remayne,
And yield for pledge my poor and captyved hart,
The which, that it from her may never start,
Let her, yf please her, bynd with adamant chayne,
And from all wandring loves, which mote pervart
His safe assurance, strongly it restrayne.
    Onely let her abstaine from cruelty,
    And doe me not before my time to dy.

## XLIII

Shall I then silent be, or shall I speake?
And if I speake, her wrath renew I shall;
And if I silent be, my hart will breake,
Or choked be with overflowing gall.
What tyranny is this, both my hart to thrall,
And eke my toung with proud restraint to tie,
That neither I may speake nor thinke at all,
But like a stupid stock in silence die!
Yet I my hart with silence secretly
Will teach to speak and my just cause to plead,
And eke mine eyes, with meek humility,
Love-learned letters to her eyes to read;
    Which her deep wit, that true harts thought can spel,
  Wil soon conceive, and learne to construe well.

## XLIV

When those renoumed noble peres of Greece
Through stubborn pride among themselves did iar,
Forgetfull of the famous golden fleece,
Then Orpheus with his harp theyr strife did bar.
But this continuall, cruell, civill warre
The which my selfe against my selfe doe make,
Whilest my weak powres of passions warreid arre,
No skill can stint, nor reason can aslake.
But when in hand my tunelesse harp I take,
Then doe I more augment my foes despight,
And griefe renew, and passions doe awake
To battaile, fresh against my selfe to fight.
    Mongst whome the more I seeke to settle peace,
    The more I fynd their malice to increace.

## XLV

Leave, Lady! in your glasse of cristall clene
Your goodly selfe for evermore to vew,
And in my selfe, (my inward selfe I meane,)
Most lively lyke behold your semblant trew.
Within my hart, though hardly it can shew
Thing so divine to vew of earthly eye,
The fayre idea of your celestiall hew
And every part remaines immortally:
And were it not that through your cruelty
With sorrow dimmed and deform'd it were,
The goodly ymage of your visnomy,
Clearer than cristall, would therein appere.
    But if your selfe in me ye playne will see,
    Remove the cause by which your fayre beames
                    darkned be.

## XLVI

When my abodes prefixed time is spent,
My cruell fayre streight bids me wend my way:
But then from heaven most hideous stormes are sent,
As willing me against her will to stay.
Whom then shall I-or heaven, or her-obay?
The heavens know best what is the best for me:
But as she will, whose will my life doth sway,
My lower heaven, so it perforce must be.
But ye high hevens, that all this sorowe see,
Sith all your tempests cannot hold me backe,
Aswage your storms, or else both you and she
Will both together me too sorely wrack.
    Enough it is for one man to sustaine
    The stormes which she alone on me doth raine.

## XLVII

Trust not the treason of those smyling lookes,
Untill ye have their guylefull traynes well tryde;
For they are lyke but unto golden hookes,
That from the foolish fish theyr bayts do hyde:
So she with flattring smyles weake harts doth guyde
Unto her love, and tempte to theyr decay;
Whome, being caught, she kills with cruell pryde,
And feeds at pleasure on the wretched pray.
Yet even whylst her bloody hands them slay,
Her eyes looke lovely, and upon them smyle,
That they take pleasure in their cruell play,
And, dying, doe themselves of payne beguyle.
    O mighty charm! which makes men love theyr bane,
    And thinck they dy with pleasure, live with payne.

## XLVIII

Innocent paper! whom too cruell hand
Did make the matter to avenge her yre,
And ere she could thy cause well understand,
Did sacrifize unto the greedy fyre,
Well worthy thou to have found better hyre
Then so bad end, for hereticks ordayned;
Yet heresy nor treason didst conspire,
But plead thy maisters cause, unjustly payned:
Whom she, all carelesse of his grief, constrayned
To utter forth the anguish of his hart,
And would not heare, when he to her complayned
The piteous passion of his dying smart.
    Yet live for ever, though against her will,
    And speake her good, though she requite it ill.

## XLIX

Fayre Cruell! why are ye so fierce and cruell?
Is it because your eyes have powre to kill?
Then know that mercy is the Mighties iewell,
And greater glory think to save then spill.
But if it be your pleasure and proud will
To shew the powre of your imperious eyes,
Then not on him that never thought you ill,
But bend your force against your enemyes.
Let them feel the utmost of your crueltyes,
And kill with looks, as cockatrices do:
But him that at your footstoole humbled lies,
With mercifull regard give mercy to.
    Such mercy shall you make admyr'd to be;
    So shall you live, by giving life to me.

L

Long languishing in double malady
Of my harts wound and of my bodies griefe,
There came to me a leach, that would apply
Fit medcines for my bodies best reliefe.
Vayne man, quoth I, that hast but little priefe
In deep discovery of the mynds disease;
Is not the hart of all the body chiefe,
And rules the members as it selfe doth please?
Then with some cordialls seeke for to appease
The inward languor of my wounded hart,
And then my body shall have shortly ease.
But such sweet cordialls passe physicians art:
    Then, my lyfes leach! doe you your skill reveale,
    And with one salve both hart and body heale.

## LI

Doe I not see that fayrest ymages
Of hardest marble are of purpose made,
For that they should endure through many ages,
Ne let theyr famous moniments to fade?
Why then doe I, untrainde in lovers trade,
Her hardnes blame, which I should more commend?
Sith never ought was excellent assayde
Which was not hard t'atchive and bring to end;
Ne ought so hard, but he that would attend
Mote soften it and to his will allure.
So do I hope her stubborne hart to bend,
And that it then more stedfast will endure:
    Only my paines wil be the more to get her;
    But, having her, my joy wil be the greater.

## LII

So oft as homeward I from her depart,
I go lyke one that, having lost the field,
Is prisoner led away with heavy hart,
Despoyld of warlike armes and knowen shield.
So doe I now my self a prisoner yield
To sorrow and to solitary paine,
From presence of my dearest deare exylde,
Long-while alone in languor to remaine.
There let no thought of joy, or pleasure vaine,
Dare to approch, that may my solace breed;
Bet sudden dumps, and drery sad disdayne
Of all worlds gladnesse, more my torment feed.
    So I her absens will my penaunce make,
      That of her presens I my meed may take.

## LIII

The panther, knowing that his spotted hyde
Doth please all beasts, but that his looks them fray,
Within a bush his dreadful head doth hide,
To let them gaze, whylst he on them may pray.
Right so my cruell fayre with me doth play;
For with the goodly semblance of her hew
She doth allure me to mine owne decay,
And then no mercy will unto me shew.
Great shame it is, thing so divine in view,
Made for to be the worlds most ornament,
To make the bayte her gazers to embrew:
Good shames to be to ill an instrument!
    But mercy doth with beautie best agree,
    As in theyr Maker ye them best may see.

## LIV

Of this worlds theatre in which we stay,
My Love, like the spectator, ydly sits,
Beholding me, that all the pageants play,
Disguysing diversly my troubled wits.
Sometimes I joy when glad occasion fits,
And mask in myrth lyke to a comedy:
Soone after, when my joy to sorrow flits,
I waile, and make my woes a tragedy.
Yet she, beholding me with constant eye,
Delights not in my merth, nor rues my smart:
But when I laugh, she mocks; and when I cry,
She laughs, and hardens evermore her hart.
    What then can move her? If nor merth, nor mone,
    She is no woman, but a sencelesse stone.

## LV

So oft as I her beauty doe behold,
And therewith doe her cruelty compare,
I marvaile of what substance was the mould
The which her made attonce so cruell faire.
Not earth; for her high thoughts more heavenly are:
Not water; for her love doth burne like fyre:
Not ayre; for she is not so light or rare;
Not fyre; for she doth friese with faint desire.
Then needs another element inquire,
Whereof she mote be made; that is, the skye.
For to the heaven her haughty looks aspire,
And eke her love is pure immortall hye.
    Then sith to heaven ye lykened are the best,
    Be lyke in mercy as in all the rest.

## LVI

Fayre ye be sure, but cruell and unkind,
As is a tygre, that with greedinesse
Hunts after bloud; when he by chance doth find
A feeble beast, doth felly him oppresse.
Fayre be ye sure, but proud and pitilesse,
As is a storme, that all things doth prostrate;
Finding a tree alone all comfortlesse,
Beats on it strongly, it to ruinate.
Fayre be ye sure, but hard and obstinate,
As is a rocke amidst the raging floods;
Gaynst which a ship, of succour desolate,
Doth suffer wreck both of her selfe and goods.
    That ship, that tree, and that same beast, am I,
    Whom ye doe wreck, doe ruine, and destroy.

## LVII

Sweet warriour! when shall I have peace with you?
High time it is this warre now ended were,
Which I no lenger can endure to sue,
Ne your incessant battry more to beare.
So weake my powres, so sore my wounds, appear,
That wonder is how I should live a iot,
Seeing my hart through-launced every where
With thousand arrowes which your eyes have shot.
Yet shoot ye sharpely still, and spare me not,
But glory thinke to make these cruel stoures.
Ye cruell one! what glory can be got,
In slaying him that would live gladly yours?
    Make peace therefore, and graunt me timely grace,
    That al my wounds will heale in little space.

## LVIII

*By her that is most assured to her selfe.*

Weake is th'assurance that weake flesh reposeth
In her own powre, and scorneth others ayde;
That soonest fals, when as she most supposeth
Her selfe assur'd, and is of nought affrayd,
All flesh is frayle, and all her strength unstayd,
Like a vaine bubble blowen up with ayre:
Devouring tyme and changeful chance have prayd
Her glorious pride, that none may it repayre.
Ne none so rich or wise, so strong or fayre,
But fayletb, trusting on his owne assurance:
And he that standeth on the hyghest stayre
Fals lowest; for on earth nought hath endurance.
    Why then doe ye, proud fayre, misdeeme so farre,
    That to your selfe ye most assured arre!

## LIX

Thrise happie she that is so well assured
Unto her selfe, and setled so in hart,
That neither will for better be allured,
Ne feard with worse to any chaunce to start:
But, like a steddy ship, doth strongly part
The raging waves, and kcepes her course aright,
Ne ought for tempest doth from it depart,
Ne ought for fayrer weathers false delight.
Such selfe-assurance need not feare the spight
Of grudging foes, ne favour seek of friends:
But in the stay of her owne stedfast might,
Neither to one her selfe nor other bends.
    Most happy she that most assur'd doth rest;
    But he most happy who such one loves best.

## LX

They that in course of heavenly spheares are skild
To every planet point his sundry yeare,
In which her circles voyage is fulfild:
As Mars in threescore yeares doth run his spheare.
So, since the winged god his planet cleare
Began in me to move, one yeare is spent;
The which doth longer unto me appeare,
Then al those fourty which my life out-went.
Then, by that count which lovers books invent,
The spheare of Cupid fourty yeares containes,
Which I have wasted in long languishment,
That seem'd the longer for my greater paines.
    But let my Loves fayre planet short her wayes
    This yeare ensuing, or else short my dayes.

## LXI

The glorious image of the Makers beautie,
My soverayne saynt, the idoll of my thought,
Dare not henceforth, above the bounds of dewtie,
T'accuse of pride, or rashly blame for ought.
For being, as she is, divinely wrought,
And of the brood of angels heavenly born,
And with the crew of blessed saynts upbrought,
Each of which did her with theyr guifts adorne,
The bud of joy, the blossome of the morne,
The beame of light, whom mortal eyes admyre,
What reason is it then but she should scorne
Base things, that to her love too bold aspire!
    Such heavenly formes ought rather worshipt be,
    Then dare be lov'd by men of meane degree.

## LXII

The weary yeare his race now having run,
The new begins his compast course anew:
With shew of morning mylde he bath begun,
Betokening peace and plenty to ensew.
So let us, which this chaunge of weather vew,
Chaunge eke our mynds, and former lives amend;
The old yeares sinnes forepast let us eschew,
And fly the faults with which we did offend.
Then shall the new yeares joy forth freshly send
Into the glooming world his gladsome ray,
And all these stormes, which now his beauty blend,
Shall turne to calmes, and tymely cleare away.
    So, likewise, Love! cheare you your heavy spright,
    And chaunge old yeares annoy to new delight.

## LXIII

After long stormes and tempests sad assay,
Which hardly I endured heretofore,
In dread of death, and daungerous dismay,
With which my silly bark was tossed sore,
I doe at length descry the happy shore,
In which I hope ere long for to arryve:
Fayre soyle it seemes from far, and fraught with store
Of all that deare and daynty is alyve.
Most happy he that can at last atchyve
The joyous safety of so sweet a rest;
Whose least delight sufficeth to deprive
Remembrance of all paines which him opprest.
    All paines are nothing in respect of this;
    All sorrowes short that gaine eternall blisse.

## LXIV

Comming to kisse her lyps, (such grace I found,)
Me seemd I smelt a gardin of sweet flowres,
That dainty odours from them threw around,
For damzels fit to decke their lovers bowres.
Her lips did smell lyke unto gillyflowers;
Her ruddy cheekes lyke unto roses red;
Her snowy browes lyke budded bellamoures;
Her lovely eyes lyke pincks but newly spred;
Her goodly bosome lyke a strawberry bed;
Her neck lyke to a bounch of cullambynes;
Her brest lyke lillyes, ere their leaves be shed;
Her nipples lyke young blossomd jessemynes.
    Such fragrant flowres doe give most odorous smell;
    But her sweet odour did them all excell.

## LXV

The doubt which ye misdeeme, fayre Love, is vaine,
That fondly feare to lose your liberty,
When, losing one, two liberties ye gayne,
And make him bond that bondage earst did fly.
Sweet be the bands the which true love doth tye,
Without constraynt or dread of any ill:
The gentle birde feeles no captivity
Within her cage, but sings, and feeds her fill.
There pride dare not approch, nor discord spill
The league twixt them that loyal love hath bound,
But simple Truth and mutual Good-will
Seeks with sweet peace to salve each others wound:
    There Fayth doth fearless dwell in brasen towre,
    And spotlesse Pleasure builds her sacred bowre.

## LXVI

To all those happy blessings which ye have
With plenteous hand by heaven upon you thrown,
This one disparagement they to you gave,
That ye your love lent to so meane a one.
Ye, whose high worths surpassing paragon
Could not on earth have found one fit for mate,
Ne but in heaven matchable to none,
Why did ye stoup unto so lowly state?
But ye thereby much greater glory gate,
Then had ye sorted with a princes pere:
For now your light doth more it selfe dilate,
And, in my darknesse, greater doth appeare.
    Yet, since your light hath once enlumind me,
    With my reflex yours shall encreased be.

## LXVII

Lyke as a huntsman, after weary chace,
Seeing the game from him escapt away,
Sits downe to rest him in some shady place,
With panting hounds, beguiled of their pray,
So, after long pursuit and vaine assay,
When I all weary had the chace forsooke,
The gentle deer returnd the selfe-same way,
Thinking to quench her thirst at the next brooke.
There she, beholding me with mylder looke,
Sought not to fly, but fearlesse still did bide,
Till I in hand her yet halfe trembling tooke,
And with her own goodwill her fyrmely tyde.
    Strange thing, me seemd, to see a beast so wyld
    So goodly wonne, with her owne will beguyld.

## LXVIII

Most glorious Lord of lyfe! that on this day
Didst make thy triumph over death and sin,
And, having harrowd hell, didst bring away
Captivity thence captive, us to win,
This joyous day, dear Lord, with joy begin;
And grant that we, for whom thou diddest dy,
Being with thy deare blood clene washt from sin,
May live for ever in felicity;
And that thy love we weighing worthily,
May likewise love thee for the same againe,
And for thy sake, that all lyke deare didst buy.
With love may one another entertayne!
    So let us love, deare Love, lyke as we ought:
    Love is the lesson which the Lord us taught.

## LXIX

The famous warriors of the anticke world
Us'd trophees to erect in stately wize,
In which they would the records have enrold
Of theyr great deeds and valorous emprize.
What trophee then shall I most fit devize,
In which I may record the memory
Of my loves conquest, peerlesse beauties prise,
Adorn'd with honour, love, and chastity!
Even this verse, vowd to eternity,
Shall be thereof immortall moniment,
And tell her praise to all posterity,
That may admire such worlds rare wonderment;
    The happy purchase of my glorious spoile,
    Gotten at last with labour and long toyle.

## LXX

Fresh Spring, the herald of loves mighty king,
In whose cote-armour richly are displayd
All sorts of flowres the which on earth do spring,
In goodly colours gloriously arrayd,
Goe to my Love, where she is carelesse layd,
Yet in her winters bowre not well awake:
Tell her the joyous time wil not be staid,
Unlesse she doe him by the forelock take;
Bid her therefore her selfe soone ready make,
To wayt on Love amongst his lovely crew,
Where every one that misseth then her make
Shall be by him amearst with penance dew.
    Make haste therefore, sweet Love, while it is prime;
    For none can call againe the passed time.

## LXXI

I joy to see how, in your drawen work,
Your selfe unto the Bee ye doe compare,
And me unto the Spyder, that doth lurke
In close awayt, to catch her unaware.
Right so your selfe were caught in cunning snare
Of a deare foe, and thralled to his love;
In whose streight bands ye now captived are
So firmely, that ye never may remove.
But as your worke is woven all about
With woodbynd flowers and fragrant eglantine,
So sweet your prison you in time shall prove,
With many deare delights bedecked fyne:
    And all thensforth eternall peace shall see
    Betweene the Spyder and the gentle Bee.

## LXXII

Oft when my spirit doth spred her bolder winges,
In mind to mount up to the purest sky,
It down is weighd with thought of earthly things,
And clogd with burden of mortality:
Where, when that soverayne beauty it doth spy,
Resembling heavens glory in her light,
Drawn with sweet pleasures bayt it back doth fly,
And unto heaven forgets her former flight.
There my fraile fancy, fed with full delight,
Doth bathe in blisse, and mantlcth most at ease;
Ne thinks of other heaven, but how it might
Her harts desire with most contentment please.
    Hart need not wish none other happinesse,
    But here on earth to have such hevens blisse.

## LXXIII

Being my self captyved here in care,
My hart, (whom none with servile bands can tye,
But the fayre tresses of your golden hayre,)
Breaking his prison, forth to you doth fly.
Like as a byrd, that in ones hand doth spy
Desired food, to it doth make his flight,
Even so my hart, that wont on your fayre eye
To feed his fill, flyes backe unto your sight.
Doe you him take, and in your bosome bright
Gently encage, that he may be your thrall:
Perhaps he there may learne, with rare delight,
To sing your name and prayses over all:
    That it hereafter may you not repent,
    Him lodging in your bosome to have lent.

## LXXIV

Most happy letters! fram'd by skilfull trade,
With which that happy name was first desynd
The which three times thrise happy hath me made,
With guifts of body, fortune, and of mind.
The first ray being to me gave by kind,
From mothers womb deriv'd by dew descent:
The second is my sovereigne Queene most kind,
That honour and large richesse to me lent:
The third my Love, my lives last ornament,
By whom my spirit out of dust was raysed,
To speake her prayse and glory excellent,
Of all alive most worthy to be praysed.
    Ye three Elizabeths! for ever live,
    That three such graces did unto me give.

## LXXV

One day I wrote her name upon the strand,
But came the waves and washed it away:
Agayne I wrote it with a second hand;
But came the tyde, and made my paynes his pray.
"Vayne man," sayd she, "that doest in vaine assay
A mortall thing so to immortalize;
For I my selve shall lyke to this decay,
And eke my name bee wyped out lykewize."
"Not so," quod I; "let baser things devize
To dy in dust, but you shall live by fame:
My verse your vertues rare shall eternize,
And in the hevens wryte your glorious name.
    Where, when as death shall all the world subdew,
    Our love shall live, and later life renew."

## LXXVI

Fayre bosome! fraught with vertues richest tresure,
The neast of love, the lodging of delight,
The bowre of blisse, the paradice of pleasure,
The sacred harbour of that hevenly spright,
How was I ravisht with your lovely sight,
And my frayle thoughts too rashly led astray,
Whiles diving deepe through amorous insight,
On the sweet spoyle of beautie they did pray,
And twixt her paps, like early fruit in May,
Whose harvest seemd to hasten now apace,
They loosely did theyr wanton winges display,
And there to rest themselves did boldly place.
    Sweet thoughts! I envy your so happy rest,
    Which oft I wisht, yet never was so blest.

## LXXVII

Was it a dreame, or did I see it playne?
A goodly table of pure yvory,
All spred with juncats fit to entertayne
The greatest prince with pompous roialty:
Mongst which, there in a silver dish did ly
Two golden apples of unvalewd price,
Far passing those which Hercules came by,
Or those which Atalanta did entice;
Exceeding sweet, yet voyd of sinfull vice;
That many sought, yet none could ever taste;
Sweet fruit of pleasure, brought from Paradice
By Love himselfe, and in his garden plaste.
    Her brest that table was, so richly spredd;
    My thoughts the guests, which would thereon have
                               fedd.

## LXXVIII

Lackyng my Love, I go from place to place,
Lyke a young fawne that late hath lost the hynd,
And seeke each where where last I sawe her face,
Whose ymage yet I carry fresh in mynd.
I seeke the fields with her late footing synd;
I seeke her bowre with her late presence deckt;
Yet nor in field nor bowre I can her fynd,
Yet field and bowre are full of her aspect.
But when myne eyes I therunto direct,
They ydly back return to me agayne;
And when I hope to see theyr trew obiect,
I fynd my self but fed with fancies vayne.
    Cease then, myne eyes, to seeke her selfe to see,
    And let my thoughts behold her selfe in mee.

## LXXIX

Men call you fayre, and you doe credit it,
For that your selfe ye daily such doe see:
But the trew fayre, that is the gentle wit
And vertuous mind, is much more praysd of me.
For all the rest, how ever fayre it be,
Shall turne to nought and lose that glorious hew;
But onely that is permanent, and free
From frayle corruption that doth flesh ensew.
That is true beautie: that doth argue you
To be divine, and born of heavenly seed,
Deriv'd from that fayre Spirit from whom all true
And perfect beauty did at first proceed.
    He only fayre, and what he fayre hath made;
    All other fayre, lyke flowres, untymely fade.

## LXXXX

After so long a race as I have run
Through Faery land, which those six books compile,
Give leave to rest me being half foredonne,
And gather to my selfe new breath awhile.
Then, as a steed refreshed after toyle,
Out of my prison I will break anew,
And stoutly will that second work assoyle,
With strong endevour and attention dew.
Till then give leave to me in pleasant mew
To sport my Muse, and sing my Loves sweet praise,
The contemplation of whose heavenly hew
My spirit to an higher pitch will rayse.
    But let her prayses yet be low and meane,
      Fit for the handmayd of the Faery Queene.

# LXXXI

Fayre is my Love, when her fayre golden haires
With the loose wynd ye waving chance to marke;
Fayre, when the rose in her red cheekes appeares,
Or in her eyes the fyre of love does sparke;
Fayre, when her brest, lyke a rich laden barke,
With pretious merchandize she forth doth lay;
Fayre, when that cloud of pryde, which oft doth dark
Her goodly light, with smiles she drives away.
But fayrest she, when so she doth display
The gate with pearles and rubyes richly dight,
Throgh which her words so wise do make their way,
To beare the message of her gentle spright.
    The rest be works of Natures wonderment;
    But this the worke of harts astonishment.

## LXXXII

Ioy of my life! full oft for loving you
I blesse my lot, that was so lucky placed:
But then the more your owne mishap I rew,
That are so much by so meane love embased.
For had the equall hevens so much you graced
In this as in the rest, ye mote invent
Some hevenly wit, whose verse could have enchased
Your glorious name in golden moniment.
But since ye deignd so goodly to relent
To me your thrall, in whom is little worth,
That little that I am shall all be spent
In setting your immortal prayses forth:
    Whose lofty argument, uplifting me,
    Shall lift you up unto an high degree.

## LXXXIII

Let not one sparke of filthy lustfull fyre
Breake out, that may her sacred peace molest;
Ne one light glance of sensuall desyre
Attempt to work her gentle mindes unrest:
But pure affections bred in spotlesse brest,
And modest thoughts breathd from well-tempred
                              spirits,
Goe visit her in her chaste bowre of rest,
Accompanyde with angelick delightes.
There fill your selfe with those most joyous sights,
The which my selfe could never yet attayne:
But speake no word to her of these sad plights,
Which her too constant stiffnesse doth constrayn.
    Onely behold her rare perfection,
    And blesse your fortunes fayre election.

## LXXXIV

The world, that cannot deeme of worthy things,
When I doe praise her, say I doe but flatter:
So does the cuckow, when the mavis sings,
Begin his witlesse note apace to clatter.
But they, that skill not of so heavenly matter,
All that they know not, envy or admyre;
Rather then envy, let them wonder at her,
But not to deeme of her desert aspyre.
Deepe in the closet of my parts entyre,
Her worth is written with a golden quill,
That me with heavenly fury doth inspire,
And my glad mouth with her sweet prayses fill:
    Which when as Fame in her shril trump shall thunder,
    Let the world chuse to envy or to wonder.

## LXXXV

Venemous tongue, tipt with vile adders sting,
Of that self kynd with which the Furies fell,
Their snaky heads doe combe, from which a spring
Of poysoned words and spightfull speeches well,
Let all the plagues and horrid paines of hell
Upon thee fall for thine accursed hyre,
That with false forged lyes, which thou didst tell.
In my true Love did stirre up coles of yre:
The sparkes whereof let kindle thine own fyre,
And, catching hold on thine own wicked bed,
Consume thee quite, that didst with guile conspire
In my sweet peace such breaches to have bred!
    Shame be thy meed, and mischiefe thy reward,
    Due to thy selfe, that it for me prepard!

## LXXXVI

Since I did leave the presence of my Love,
Many long weary dayes I have outworne,
And many nights, that slowly seemd to move
Theyr sad protract from evening untill morn.
For, when as day the heaven doth adorne,
I wish that night the noyous day would end:
And when as night hath us of light forlorne,
I wish that day would shortly reascend.
Thus I the time with expectation spend,
And faine my griefe with chaunges to beguile,
That further seemes his terme still to extend,
And maketh every minute seem a myle.
    So sorrowe still doth seem too long to last;
    But joyous houres do fly away too fast.

## LXXXVII

Since I have lackt the comfort of that light
The which was wont to lead my thoughts astray,
I wander as in darknesse of the night,
Affrayd of every dangers least dismay.
Ne ought I see, though in the clearest day,
When others gaze upon theyr shadowes vayne,
But th'only image of that heavenly ray
Whereof some glance doth in mine eie remayne.
Of which beholding the idaea playne,
Through contemplation of my purest part,
With light thereof I doe my self sustayne,
And thereon feed my love-affamisht hart.
    But with such brightnesse whylest I fill my mind,
    I starve my body, and mine eyes doe blynd.

## LXXXVIII

Lyke as the culver on the bared bough
Sits mourning for the absence of her mate,
And in her songs sends many a wishful vow
For his returns, that seemes to linger late,
So I alone, how left disconsolate,
Mourne to my selfe the absence of my Love;
And wandring here and there all desolate,
Seek with my playnts to match that mournful dove
Ne joy of ought that under heaven doth hove,
Can comfort me, but her owne joyous sight,
Whose sweet aspect both God and man can move,
In her unspotted pleasauns to delight.
    Dark is my day, whyles her fayre light I mis,
    And dead my life that wants such lively blis.

NOTE

I have opted to let the *Amoretti* poems stand alone, without an introduction. There are many studies of Edmund Spenser's poetry available.

I have provided some further reading for Spenser's work, and for the art of the Elizabethan sonnet below.

For books on the sonnet, those by Michael Spiller and Sandra Berman are excellent. Heather Dubrow's study of the sonnet form and the influence of Francesco Petrarch on English poetry is superb. J.W. Lever's and Maurice Valency's books are classics.

FURTHER READING

Sandra Berman. *The Sonnet Over Time*, Chapel Hill, 1988

Jean R. Brink *et al*, eds: *The Politics of Gender in Early Modern, Sixteenth Century Studies and Essays*, 12, 1989

Reed Way Dasenbrock. *Imitating the Italians: Wyatt, Spenser, Syne, Pound, Joyce*, John Hopkins University Press, Baltimore, 1991

Stevie Davies: *The Idea of Woman in Renaissance Literature: The Feminine Reclaimed*, Harvester Press, Brighton 1986

Heather Dubrow. *Echoes of Desire: English Petrarchism and Its Counterdiscourses,* Cornell University Press, 1995

Maurice Evans, ed. *Elizabethan Sonnets*, Dent, 1977

Margaret Ferguson. *Trials of Desire: Renaissance Defenses of Poetry*, Yale University Press, New Haven, 1983

—. *et al*, eds. *Rewriting the Renaissance*, University of Chicago Press, 1986

Anne Ferry. *The "Inward" Language: Sonnets of Wyatt, Sidney, Shakespeare, Donne*, University of Chicago Press, 1983

William P. Haugaard: *Elizabeth and the English Reformation: The Struggle for a Stable Settlement of Religion*, Cambridge University Press, 1968

Jane Hedley. *Power in Verse: Metaphor and Metonymy in the Renaissance Lyric*, Pennsylvania State University Press University

Park, 1988

J.W. Lever. *The Elizabethan Love Sonnet*, Methuen, 1956

Arthur Marotti. ""Love is not love": Elizabethan Sonnet Sequences and the Social Order", *English Literary History*, 49, 1982

Louise Montrose: ""Eliza, Queene of Shepheardes" and the Pastoral of Power", in *English Language Review*, vol. X, 1980, 164-6

Adrian Morey: *The Catholic Subjects of Elizabeth I*, Allen & Unwin 1978

Maureen Sabine: *Feminine Engendered Faith: The Poetry of John Donne and Richard Crashaw*, Macmillan 1992

Michael R.G. Spiller: *The Development of the Sonnet: An introduction*, Routledge 1992

Roy Strong: *The Cult of Elizabeth I*, Thames & Hudson 1977

Leonard Tennenhouse: *Power on Display: The Politics of Shakespeare's Genres*, Methuen 1986

Maurice Valency. *In Praise of Love: An Introduction to the Love-Poetry of the Renaissance*, Macmillan, New York, 1961

Robin Wells: *Spenser's Faerie Queene and the Cult of Elizabeth*, Barnes & Noble, Totowa, New Jersey 1983

Elkin Calhoun Wilson: *England's Eliza*, Harvard Studies in English, vol. XX, Octagon, New York 1966

# CRESCENT MOON PUBLISHING

web: www.crmoon.com  e-mail: cresmopub@yahoo.co.uk

## ARTS, PAINTING, SCULPTURE

The Art of Andy Goldsworthy
Andy Goldsworthy: Touching Nature
Andy Goldsworthy in Close-Up
Andy Goldsworthy: Pocket Guide
Andy Goldsworthy In America
Land Art: A Complete Guide
The Art of Richard Long
Richard Long: Pocket Guide
Land Art In the UK
Land Art in Close-Up
Land Art In the U.S.A.
Land Art: Pocket Guide
Installation Art in Close-Up
Minimal Art and Artists In the 1960s and After
Colourfield Painting
Land Art DVD, TV documentary
Andy Goldsworthy DVD, TV documentary
The Erotic Object: Sexuality in Sculpture From Prehistory to the Present Day
Sex in Art: Pornography and Pleasure in Painting and Sculpture
Postwar Art
Sacred Gardens: The Garden in Myth, Religion and Art
Glorification: Religious Abstraction in Renaissance and 20th Century Art
Early Netherlandish Painting
Leonardo da Vinci
Piero della Francesca
Giovanni Bellini
Fra Angelico: Art and Religion in the Renaissance
Mark Rothko: The Art of Transcendence
Frank Stella: American Abstract Artist
Jasper Johns
Brice Marden
Alison Wilding: The Embrace of Sculpture
Vincent van Gogh: Visionary Landscapes
Eric Gill: Nuptials of God
Constantin Brancusi: Sculpting the Essence of Things
Max Beckmann
Caravaggio
Gustave Moreau
Egon Schiele: Sex and Death In Purple Stockings
Delizioso Fotografico Fervore: Works In Process 1
Sacro Cuore: Works In Process 2
The Light Eternal: J.M.W. Turner
The Madonna Glorified: Karen Arthurs

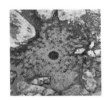

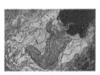

# LITERATURE

J.R.R. Tolkien: The Books, The Films, The Whole Cultural Phenomenon
J.R.R. Tolkien: Pocket Guide
Tolkien's Heroic Quest
The *Earthsea* Books of Ursula Le Guin
Beauties, Beasts and Enchantment: Classic French Fairy Tales
German Popular Stories by the Brothers Grimm
Philip Pullman and *His Dark Materials*
Sexing Hardy: Thomas Hardy and Feminism
Thomas Hardy's *Tess of the d'Urbervilles*
Thomas Hardy's *Jude the Obscure*
Thomas Hardy: The Tragic Novels
Love and Tragedy: Thomas Hardy
The Poetry of Landscape in Hardy
Wessex Revisited: Thomas Hardy and John Cowper Powys
Wolfgang Iser: Essays and Interviews
Petrarch, Dante and the Troubadours
Maurice Sendak and the Art of Children's Book Illustration
Andrea Dworkin
Cixous, Irigaray, Kristeva: The *Jouissance* of French Feminism
Julia Kristeva: Art, Love, Melancholy, Philosophy, Semiotics and Psychoanalysis
Hélene Cixous I Love You: The *Jouissance* of Writing
Luce Irigaray: Lips, Kissing, and the Politics of Sexual Difference
Peter Redgrove: Here Comes the Flood
Peter Redgrove: Sex-Magic-Poetry-Cornwall
Lawrence Durrell: Between Love and Death, East and West
Love, Culture & Poetry: Lawrence Durrell
Cavafy: Anatomy of a Soul
German Romantic Poetry: Goethe, Novalis, Heine, Hölderlin
Feminism and Shakespeare
Shakespeare: Love, Poetry & Magic
The Passion of D.H. Lawrence
D.H. Lawrence: Symbolic Landscapes
D.H. Lawrence: Infinite Sensual Violence
Rimbaud: Arthur Rimbaud and the Magic of Poetry
The Ecstasies of John Cowper Powys
Sensualism and Mythology: The Wessex Novels of John Cowper Powys
Amorous Life: John Cowper Powys and the Manifestation of Affectivity (H.W. Fawkner)
Postmodern Powys: New Essays on John Cowper Powys (Joe Boulter)
Rethinking Powys: Critical Essays on John Cowper Powys
Paul Bowles & Bernardo Bertolucci
Rainer Maria Rilke
Joseph Conrad: *Heart of Darkness*
In the Dim Void: Samuel Beckett
Samuel Beckett Goes into the Silence
André Gide: Fiction and Fervour
Jackie Collins and the Blockbuster Novel
Blinded By Her Light: The Love-Poetry of Robert Graves
The Passion of Colours: Travels In Mediterranean Lands
Poetic Forms

## POETRY

Ursula Le Guin: Walking In Cornwall
Peter Redgrove: Here Comes The Flood
Peter Redgrove: Sex-Magic-Poetry-Cornwall
Dante: Selections From the Vita Nuova
Petrarch, Dante and the Troubadours
William Shakespeare: Sonnets
William Shakespeare: Complete Poems
Blinded By Her Light: The Love-Poetry of Robert Graves
Emily Dickinson: Selected Poems
Emily Brontë: Poems
Thomas Hardy: Selected Poems
Percy Bysshe Shelley: Poems
John Keats: Selected Poems
Joh n Keats: Poems of 1820
D.H. Lawrence: Selected Poems
Edmund Spenser: Poems
Edmund Spenser: Amoretti
John Donne: Poems
Henry Vaughan: Poems
Sir Thomas Wyatt: Poems
Robert Herrick: Selected Poems
Rilke: Space, Essence and Angels in the Poetry of Rainer Maria Rilke
Rainer Maria Rilke: Selected Poems
Friedrich Hölderlin: Selected Poems
Arseny Tarkovsky: Selected Poems
Arthur Rimbaud: Selected Poems
Arthur Rimbaud: A Season in Hell
Arthur Rimbaud and the Magic of Poetry
Novalis: Hymns To the Night
German Romantic Poetry
Paul Verlaine: Selected Poems
Elizaethan Sonnet Cycles
D.J. Enright: By-Blows
Jeremy Reed: Brigitte's Blue Heart
Jeremy Reed: Claudia Schiffer's Red Shoes
Gorgeous Little Orpheus
Radiance: New Poems
Crescent Moon Book of Nature Poetry
Crescent Moon Book of Love Poetry
Crescent Moon Book of Mystical Poetry
Crescent Moon Book of Elizabethan Love Poetry
Crescent Moon Book of Metaphysical Poetry
Crescent Moon Book of Romantic Poetry
Pagan America: New American Poetry

## MEDIA, CINEMA, FEMINISM and CULTURAL STUDIES

J.R.R. Tolkien: The Books, The Films, The Whole Cultural Phenomenon
J.R.R. Tolkien: Pocket Guide
The *Lord of the Rings* Movies: Pocket Guide
The Cinema of Hayao Miyazaki
Hayao Miyazaki: *Princess Mononoke*: Pocket Movie Guide
Hayao Miyazaki: *Spirited Away*: Pocket Movie Guide
Tim Burton : Hallowe'en For Hollywood
Ken Russell
Ken Russell: *Tommy*: Pocket Movie Guide
The Ghost Dance: The Origins of Religion
The Peyote Cult
Cixous, Irigaray, Kristeva: The *Jouissance* of French Feminism
Julia Kristeva: Art, Love, Melancholy, Philosophy, Semiotics and Psychoanalysis
Luce Irigaray: Lips, Kissing, and the Politics of Sexual Difference
Hélene Cixous I Love You: The *Jouissance* of Writing
Andrea Dworkin
'Cosmo Woman': The World of Women's Magazines
Women in Pop Music
HomeGround: The Kate Bush Anthology
Discovering the Goddess (Geoffrey Ashe)
The Poetry of Cinema
The Sacred Cinema of Andrei Tarkovsky
Andrei Tarkovsky: Pocket Guide
Andrei Tarkovsky: *Mirror*: Pocket Movie Guide
Andrei Tarkovsky: *The Sacrifice*: Pocket Movie Guide
Walerian Borowczyk: Cinema of Erotic Dreams
Jean-Luc Godard: The Passion of Cinema
Jean-Luc Godard: *Hail Mary*: Pocket Movie Guide
Jean-Luc Godard: *Contempt*: Pocket Movie Guide
Jean-Luc Godard: *Pierrot le Fou*: Pocket Movie Guide
John Hughes and Eighties Cinema
*Ferris Bueller's Day Off*: Pocket Movie Guide
Jean-Luc Godard: Pocket Guide
The Cinema of Richard Linklater
Liv Tyler: Star In Ascendance
*Blade Runner* and the Films of Philip K. Dick
Paul Bowles and Bernardo Bertolucci
Media Hell: Radio, TV and the Press
An Open Letter to the BBC
Detonation Britain: Nuclear War in the UK
Feminism and Shakespeare
Wild Zones: Pornography, Art and Feminism
Sex in Art: Pornography and Pleasure in Painting and Sculpture
Sexing Hardy: Thomas Hardy and Feminism

*The Light Eternal* is a model monograph, an exemplary job. The subject matter of the book is beautifully organised and dead on beam. (Lawrence Durrell)

It is amazing for me to see my work treated with such passion and respect. (Andrea Dworkin)

**CRESCENT MOON PUBLISHING**
P.O. Box 1312, Maidstone, Kent, ME14 5XU, Great Britain. www.crmoon.com

cresmopub@yahoo.co.uk    www.crescentmoon.org.uk

Made in the USA
Middletown, DE
16 May 2016